# FENG SHUI

# FACTS & MYTHS

By Larry Sang
Translated by Sylvia Lam
Edited by Chris Shaul and Lorraine Wilcox
Cover Designed by Mika Yu

Original Title : Feng Shui Facts and Myths

Published by: American Feng Shui Institute

Address:       108 North Ynez Avenue, Suite 202

               Monterey Park, California 91754

Email:         fsinfo@amfengshui.com

Website:       www.amfengshui.com

Writer: Larry Sang
Translater: Sylvia Lam
Editor: Chris Shaul  and  Lorraine Wilcox
Cover Design and Layout :  Mika Yu

# ACKNOWLEDGEMENTS

My thanks go first to Sylvia Lam who translated Feng Shui Facts & Myths into English for me, and to Chris Shaul for his patience in editing.

I also greatly appreciate to Mika Yu for her elegant graphic design, which adds substantial comprehension and illustrates my work.

More thanks than I can express here go to Lorraine Wilcox, who put together and polished the draft of the translation. Without her care and thoughtfulness, the publication of this book would not have been so smooth.

# ABOUT THE AUTHOR

Larry Sang is the founder of the American Feng Shui Institute. The Institute was established in 1991, headquartered in Monterey Park, California. The American Feng Shui Institute teaches all aspects of the Chinese Five Arts: Feng Shui, Yi Jing, Four Pillars, Zi Wei Dou Shu, and Palm and Face Reading.

Larry Sang is one of the most influential practitioners in the philosophy and teachings of Feng Shui. He has a Ph.D. for his work in transcribing the Yi Jing. His work is recognized globally by clients, students and other Feng Shui practitioners, Fortune 500 companies and governments from Asia to the United States.

 *Table of Contents*

# Contents

*Painted by Larry Sang*

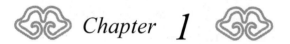 *Chapter* *1*

# Feng Shui Study:
## Scientific or Superstitious?

Wherever Chinese people dwell - China, Hong Kong, Taiwan, Singapore, Malaysia, etc., even in Europe and America - there are always swindlers using Feng Shui as a tool to cheat people. Because of this, many confuse Feng Shui and the study of destiny with the methods of these swindlers, who often mix in religious practices.

The confusion is understandable, but the result is quite unfair to practitioners of classical Feng Shui. The consumer should know that one who practices Feng Shui and fate calculation does not need to be a follower of the Buddha or the gods.

There are only a few who know Chinese metaphysics, and even fewer are acquainted with this knowledge in depth. A skilled master is as rare as a phoenix feather or a unicorn horn.

Fakers can easily make a marketable product to cheat the public. A Chinese saying calls this mixing fish eyes with pearls Perhaps this needs a little explanation. Both fish eyes and pearls are small white spheres, but one is of value and the other is quite cheap.

General practitioners of these 'arts' can easily fool others by babbling about their 'knowledge' of Feng Shui and destiny. Just as medicine was originally a respected profession, yet today we hear that some doctors have cheated their patients. Of course, we should not blame all doctors because of a few bad one.

Feng Shui Study is unique in Chinese culture. It lies between superstition and fact; it is scientific, but not totally so. Its practice has become attached to the common person's belief in gods, ghosts, and spirits. This wraps Feng Shui in mysterious colors.

From the late Qing dynasty (which ended 1911) until now, many Chinese scholars have despised "Kan Yu" (an old name for Feng Shui). It has come to be looked upon in the East as superstitious and as a tool for swindlers to cheat people.

Yet today, Feng Shui flourishes in the West. A lot of scholars have joined in this research. Nowadays, many people have restricted their thoughts to the 'scientific standard.' Feng Shui is difficult to prove by this standard, since it depends on the interaction between environment, direction, time, space, and people. Good fortune and bad fortune float between these interconnected factors. Modern science cannot measure such a complex interaction.

The five arts of Chinese metaphysics include medicine, divination, astrology, appraisal by appearance, and mountain. Divination is mainly the study of the Yi Jing. Appraisal by appearance is things like palm and face reading. Mountain includes the Feng Shui of the environment.

Among the five arts of Chinese metaphysics, medicine is the most commonly used in modern life. Similar to Feng Shui, Chinese medicine is based on the five elements, which generate and reduce each other in cycles. In time, scientists have accepted Chinese medicine because people have researched it and dedicated themselves to its study. In the future, deeper research and analysis of Feng Shui will bring its acceptance. I believe that one day the mysterious spell surrounding it shall be broken.

In 1991, I was a guest professor at the University of Southern California, teaching a six-week Feng Shui class. Upon completion, the University issued certificates for the students. The course was in English. Since then, I have taught at different universities and established the *American Feng Shui Institute* in Monterey

Park. Thousands of students from all walks of life, from Europe and America, have attended these classes. Those who have participated have learned how to practice Feng Shui and to understand the balance of yin and yang. They have learned how to use the five elements – metal, wood, water, fire and earth – to capture or reduce the strong and the weak qi. Furthermore, they have learned how to use the qi, how to use their new knowledge to search for a good environment, and how to analyze good and bad fortune.

Classical Feng Shui has two parts: the qi and the environment. To learn the 'qi' is to study the four directions (north, east, south, west), the four corners (southeast, southwest, northeast, northwest), and the center. It is learning the relationship of the five elements to good and bad fortune. It is learning about the ancient Chinese diagrams: the river map (he tu) and the luo writing (luo shu). To learn qi is to study the calculation of the qi, and the movement of time.

Environment is the study of the terrain: the form of mountains, streams, and rivers. It is the layout of the city, including street alignment, the roads, and the shapes of buildings. It is the interior of the house, the partitions, the location of the door, the lighting, and colors, etc.

Feng Shui study does not involve ghosts and spirits. I do not talk about gods or ghosts during my classes. Moreover I do not practice the occult nor cultivate witch craft.

*Chapter* 2

# Feng Shui Study and Superstition

Today, science is a hot topic that people enjoy discussing, while Feng Shui is often looked upon as superstition. This negative reaction and criticism cannot totally be blamed on the partiality of the modern-minded person. Those who are practicing and researching Feng Shui must also approach it seriously. There is a Chinese saying that advises us to 'bring order out of chaos.' Practitioners must bear the burden of clearing away the superstition in their practice, so that people do not perceive Feng Shui as superstitious.

Presently, in the developed areas of the world, there are a lot of well-educated specialists, such as doctors, philosophers, engineers, astronomers, and professors who have humbly joined in the research. They take Feng Shui as the study of the living environment. They earnestly and willingly want to learn this.

From my years of experience, most of the strong critics of Feng Shui and fate calculation admit that they do not understand this field of study. They place themselves at a higher level and show signs of distaste on their faces when discussing it. One should not comment without reasonable proof of their views, especially if they do not understand it, have never experienced it, have just picked up ideas from hearsay, or have been cheated by crooks. These unfair statements only demonstrate that the speaker is the superstitious one. To distinguish between superstition and fact in science or religion, one must first understand the topic. Without investigating and acquiring a certain level of knowledge in a field, one does not have a standard to judge what is and what is not superstition.

True Feng Shui masters are few, whereas cheaters are everywhere. In a Chinese mall in San Gabriel, California, there was a large restaurant. On the instructions of a Feng Shui master, they put half-filled fish tanks on both sides of their escalator. The tanks were without fish. At the reception counter, they placed a picture of the Chinese ghost hunter, Zhong Kui, and a statue of bats, which are considered lucky in Chinese culture.

This so-called Feng Shui is ridiculous. The arrangement was removed after a short time. It is needless to say why. The next chapters will give tips on how to identify true and false Feng Shui masters.

*Painted by Larry Sang*

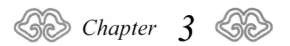 *Chapter* 3

# How to Tell a True
## from a False Feng Shui Master

Throughout the ages, whenever a product becomes famous and marketable, fakers emerge 'mixing fish eyes with pearls.'

Conjurers are quite skillful in puffing things up. They call themselves "Specialist in Kan Yu," "Feng Shui Master," "Half-Immortal," "True Man," etc. They speak of gods, spirits, and ghosts. They confuse and deceive the public. Out of the five arts (medicine, mountain, divination, astrology, and appraisal by appearance), you will find the most frauds in the art of Feng Shui. There are so many believers, but few have any knowledge. This makes fertile ground for cheating to bloom.

I estimate that 85% of Feng Shui 'masters' who put advertisements in newspapers, magazines, and on television do not understand Feng Shui at all. It is sad to say, but 85% is certainly a conservative estimate.

A skilled specialist in any one of the five arts (divination, astrology, palm and face reading, or Feng Shui) can certainly lead a very comfortable life. Business keeps rolling in. At times, one even has to refuse clients due to lack of time. Why bother spending money on advertising? This is a very simple and easy to understand point.

In the places where Chinese people reside, such as Hong Kong and Taiwan, it is common to see Feng Shui masters being interviewed on television. The contents of these interviews make real masters shake their heads sadly. In any age, whatever type of metaphysics is used, there are always limitations. Using astrological calculations to foretell the daily stock markets, the rise and fall of the foreign exchange, the results of a student or professional examination, etc. is a big blunder. This is a serious contamination of metaphysics.

A common saying among practitioners of the five arts is that "Destiny is the most important influence. Luck is second. Feng Shui is third." Feng Shui is only one of these influences, and indeed, it is the least potent one. Because of this, one's destiny can not be entirely altered by using Feng Shui.

The Chinese believe that every person has his own pre-determined destiny and luck, received from his parents and by his birth time. There is no chance to select this. Those who understand Four Pillars and Ziwei Dou Shu (two types of Chinese astrology) know why we need to make a natal astrology chart first, showing the birth time and the stars, before arranging the luck formulas. The power of Feng Shui is to adjust, by enhancing or reducing the degree of fortune and misfortune, in order to receive the maximum benefit. It is impossible to use Feng Shui to convert a common person into a national leader, or to make a poor person into a billionaire, unless it is already in their fate.

Once, in a radio broadcast, I heard a prominent religious leader criticize Feng Shui. In brief, he commented that if a Feng Shui master could bring riches, fame, longevity, and honor to others, it would not be necessary for him to perform Feng Shui readings any more. He should already have everything he wants, and would not need to work.

This Buddhist preacher is a distinguished and successful leader in his field, but the remark he made regarding Feng Shui is unfair. It is like mixing ritual practices, such as worshiping spirits, drawing talismans, reciting spells, and using straw shoes to beat paper dolls, etc., with real Buddhism. Can one say, "If a doctor treats a patient, death never visits their home?" This type of criticism does not convince me.

In all kinds of professions, there are always troublemakers promoting false brands. It is not easy to select a skilled Feng Shui master, but to differentiate between true and false is not so difficult.

The following are some suggestions for you. Feng Shui charlatans love to:

1. Perform blessings, burn incense, use the black arts, recite mantras, etc.
2. Speak of past lives, your prior hatreds and misconduct, discuss ghosts and spirits.
3. Make offerings to the year god (taisui), etc.
4. For women who have had abortions, make offerings to the spirit of their aborted fetus.
5. Hang bagua mirrors, concave or convex mirrors, place money toads, statues of elephants, calabash gourds, etc.

I do not say all the above acts are useless. Burning incense, reciting mantras or prayers, or setting up an altar for worship is a form of psychotherapy in the East. Currently, people in the West also research it. However, these things should not be mixed together and called Feng Shui.

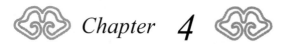 *Chapter* *4*

# How to do a Feng Shui Reading

At times, Feng Shui practitioners find themselves surrounded by people asking about their Feng Shui. The Feng Shui practitioner is the star among the crowd. Everyone opens their eyes wide and wants to know whether their home or office is in a fortunate position. An uninformed person believes that, by looking left and right, up and down, by observing north, east, south, and west with a pair of sharp eyes (or a pair of spectacles), the Feng Shui practitioner can distinguish the auspicious aspects and inauspicious signs right away.

But this is definitely not true. One must have a Luo Pan (a Chinese Feng Shui compass) when reading Feng Shui. Without a Luo Pan, even the best Feng Shui Master can not exercise his skill. Current Western publications and magazines describe me as 'Master Larry Sang, the founder of the American Feng Shui Institute, a practitioner of the Compass School.' I don't know whether to laugh or cry. How can there be a Compass School, when all true Feng Shui needs to consider the compass orientation of the building?

The main focus in reading Feng Shui is to concentrate on the surrounding environment. One must see its relationship with the structure of the building. Then from the orientation and position, we can conclude whether the building has good qi or not. The Luo Pan is an analytical tool that precisely determines the correct orientation. Without a Luo Pan, can one accurately determine if the orientation is south or southwest, north or northwest with their eyes?

In the study of Feng Shui, buildings constructed in certain periods have entirely different qi based on whether the orientation is south or southwest, north or northwest, etc. That's why, during my lectures, I frequently joke that there are only two schools of Feng Shui. One is the Compass School, while the other is the E.T. School, since only E.T.'s finger is powerful enough to pinpoint north, east, south, or west without using a Luo Pan.

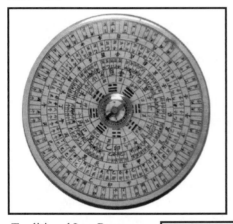

Traditional Luo Pan

Simplified Luo Pan. Sang's Luo Pan is specially designed for Westerners.

To find out whether a Feng Shui practitioner has a good level of knowledge, here are some points for you to observe:

A.) Upon arriving at the building, the practitioner should take a tour around the property to view the environment. The purpose for this is to understand the flow of qi – the good qi and the bad qi. The practitioner must determine from which direction the qi comes. He must see if the property is near a cemetery, dump site, etc. He must observe the shape of front and back of the building itself, and observe the neighbors' property, too. He must pay attention to the surrounding green-ery – whether it is luxuriant or withered, etc.

B.) The practitioner must use a Luo Pan to take an accurate reading on the sitting and facing directions. Determining the sitting direction is an essential beginning step in doing a Feng Shui reading, because even a slight mistake could result in a totally erroneous judgment of the good and evil qi. Measuring the correct sitting direction depends mainly on the experience of the practitioner.

Novices need to be accompanied and guided by mentors. They must practice on-site readings as often as possible. If the practitioner has any doubt and is without guidance, they should take two different compass readings. They then must calculate and analyze the two charts for the building. They should then match up the two charts with the past circumstances of the occupants' life to determine which one fits. The chart that appears the closest to the situation of the residents has the correct sitting direction. This is how to avoid a mistake.

Feng Shui is based mainly on sitting direction of the build-ing. I particularly want to make it clear that determining the sitting direction can be very, very difficult. Those who do not have hands-on training in how to use a Luo Pan and how to determine the sitting direction cannot know how to judge the good and bad qi.

For those schools that do not use a Luo Pan and whose Feng Shui reading does not depend on sitting direction, I will not comment on their correctness.

C.) Finding out the year of construction of the building is essential. The year of construction is the time that the roof closes off the building from the sunlight. In Feng Shui theory, the non-stop movement of the universe directly and indirectly affects the quality of the earth. Because of this, the completion year of a building's construction is part of the calculation.

A special formula is used to calculate the quality and characteristics of the qi that has been captured in the building as a whole and in the various areas of the building. This calculation results in numbers (representing stars) in nine different sections of the house. The numbers correspond to the five elements: metal, wood earth, fire, and water. Items made of the appropriate element are introduced into good areas to enhance the qi and into bad areas to remedy the not-so-good qi. This makes harmony in the building. One may also avoid the use of bad areas, if possible.

D.) The birth year of the occupants is also considered. Feng Shui theories tell us that the occupant and the house interact with each other. Therefore, the birth year and gender of an individual play a part in deciding which directions and positions bring harmony or evil.

*Painted by Larry Sang*

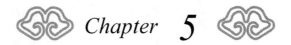

*Chapter* 5

## Schools of Feng Shui

The Eight House System Book.

Feng Shui, like the martial arts, is divided into different schools. The most popular two are 八宅風水 Ba Zhai or the Eight House system and 玄空風水 Xuan Kong or the flying star system.

The Xuan Kong Book

Their principles differ to a large extent, but they can supplement each other.

In 1991, I was the first to translate the Eight House rules into English, and I lectured on this topic at the University of Southern California. The Eight House system is the best approach for beginners to access Feng Shui.

The Xuan Kong system is also known as the 九宮飛星 Nine Palace Flying Stars. Experts in this system can perform highly accurate predictive analysis. It is a system which is difficult to learn and to manage skillfully. If one does not have a real master who is willing to hand down his knowledge, it is supremely difficult to get a hold of this art. In addition, lengthy practice is necessary. Most prominent masters are well versed in both Eight House and Xuan Kong.

There are not many who know Feng Shui thoroughly. Thus, fakers are everywhere. They create a total mess by mixing Eastern culture, customs, and superstitions with burning incense and occult arts, calling this Feng Shui.

Generally in Yang House Feng Shui (buildings for the living), bad events are caused by a harmful environment or inauspicious stars. Problems can be fixed by those who know Feng Shui. Results can be felt as quickly as three to ten days. Yin House (grave sites) requires more time after a remedy is placed to feel the results.

Besides the Eight House and Xuan Kong systems, there are other systems, such as San Yuan, San He, 64 Hexagrams, Qi Men, etc. To my understanding and experience, the other systems mainly talk about application, yet lack strong theoretical support.

Of course, there is also a lot of nonsense propagated by scholars. They develop innumerable odd styles by mixing traditional Asian habits, rituals, religious practices, and beliefs into a plate of Chinese chop suey. This utter nonsense brings disgrace to the reputation of Feng Shui.

In the United States, there are some Feng Shui practitioners who perform readings for homes and offices without even bringing along a Luo Pan. Moreover, they disregard the year the building was constructed. Their only aim is to sell ba gua mirrors, crystal balls, wind chimes, flutes, and concave and convex mirrors to their clients. Furthermore, there are those who recommend buying statues of an elephant, emphasizing that the trunk should curve to the right or left, or whatever. This is really too much. If a true master of Feng Shui does not step up to point out the folly of this type of practice, Feng Shui will go down the drain and will no longer have any credibility.

Ba gua mirrors, crystal balls, convex or concave mirrors, elephants, etc. have no meaning in Feng Shui practice. Then, if a practitioner encounters problems when assessing a place, what should he use to remedy the situation?

In Feng Shui, one applies various elements appropriate to

the situation, i.e. using metal wind chimes or metal ornaments to represent metal, red decorations or articles painted red to represent fire, and fish tanks to represent water, etc.

Each year the flying stars arrive in different positions and create specific 'currents' that usher in changes to the qi of the earth. This generates auspicious or unlucky qi. Because of this, the same element is usually not used in the same area year after year.

In dissolving sickness, obstacles, or worries in places where corrections should be made, 'Mr. Feng Shui' might give instruction to hang wind chimes as a remedy. If this is too obvious as a Feng Shui remedy, then they can be replaced with another metal ornament, such as a bronze statue, or a metal grandfather clock, etc.

Red articles, objects that are painted red, or the use of a red lampshade can stop gossip and generate money and fortune under the right circumstances.

In the right place, a fish tank or a fountain with running water can bring fortune and 'peach blossom.' Peach blossom is a Chinese term for romance, drinking, parties, and a very social life.

Some people, after reading two or three Feng Shui books, will try to practice as instructed in the books. However, their life is prone to unhappiness because they do not really know what Feng Shui is. They hang wind chimes in the entrance of a house or in the bedroom. If this were not enough, they may even hang wind chimes at each corner of the eaves of the roof. This is very dangerous. One must NOT try it. Hanging wind chimes at inappropriate places will invite disaster. If the effects are mild, it will cause bad dreams. If the effects are serious, there can be bloodshed, gun injuries, or traffic accidents. You name it!

The improper use of the color red, fish tanks, etc., can bring about a similar result. One must know about timing, the directions, and the interactions of the five elements before the application of Feng Shui remedies. Please do not try to change your luck using Feng Shui without competent advice.

Westerners do not understand Feng Shui in depth, so a lot have been hooked by charlatans. I have heard that the business of these fakers is not too bad, because they know how to present and promote themselves by advertising in the newspaper and on television. They have no worries. Customers keep rolling in.

There are a number of publications in the market that have a gorgeous cover, are beautifully bound, and adorned with colorful pictures. Those who have knowledge of Feng Shui realize that the content is shallow and the writers are mostly very poor masters or their students. The writers can not even describe the concept of yin-yang, not to mention the interrelationship of the five elements. How can one learn from such books and obtain a proper insight into Feng Shui?

One day, one of my students showed me an article from an English-language newspaper. It described how a so-called first rate Feng Shui master conducted his reading. He employed a band of musicians to beat drums and gongs, while he burnt incense and chanted mantras. If the media keeps publishing this kind of misleading news, the future of Feng Shui is at risk.

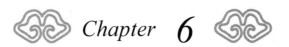 *Chapter* 6

# Feng Shui Flying Stars

Upon entering a building or house, a Feng Shui expert can instantly discover which areas create problems, if any. He can perform an Yi Jing reading on the spot and reveal what type of illness is affecting the person living in that area of the house, by using the image of the trigrams. This is a very accurate method.

In Feng Shui, the interpretation of illness is based on the combination of the trigrams and flying stars in each position. This can determine the location of the sickness sha (negative influences). The elementary formula for calculating the qi is described in my first publication, the *Principles of Feng Shui, Book 1* (published in 1994). It is also mentioned in another book written by one of my students and his wife in 1999, published by Alpha Books.

A family lives together, eating similar food, but one of them gets ill while the rest are not affected. Why? What is the reason behind this?

Analyzing from the point of view of Feng Shui, it is because every area of the house has its own qi. Bad energy residing in a certain area brings illness to people spending time there, whereas in other areas, the qi is normal. This is why only the person staying in the area with sha has poor health.

The numbers 1 through 9 are used by the Xuan Kong school of Feng Shui, and these numbers represent the nine flying stars. After determining the sitting and facing direction of the building, the number representing the time period that the construction was completed is marked in the central sector of a three by three grid. Then the stars are floated in the other eight directions. The number combinations predict what will happen. Each of the nine numbers or stars has a color and meaning:

| Number | Color | Name | |
|--------|-------|------|---|
| 1 | White | Tan Lang | 貪狼 |
| 2 | Black | Ju Men | 巨門 |
| 3 | Jade | Lu Cun | 祿存 |
| 4 | Green | Wen Qu | 文曲 |
| 5 | Yellow | Lian Zhen | 廉貞 |
| 6 | White | Wu Qu | 武曲 |
| 7 | Red | Po Jun | 破軍 |
| 8 | White | Zuo Fu | 左輔 |
| 9 | Purple | You Bi | 右弼 |

Wherever and whenever the 2 black star flies in, it symbolizes trouble from sickness or lawsuit. If 2 black and 1 white stay in the same area, and the front door or the master bedroom is located there, divorce is often the result. How can one resolve this phenomenon? It is not as simple as hanging a mirror or crystal ball.

If 2 black flies into the northeast and meets 8 white, the circumstances of the residents will be dramatically different. This combination brings wealth. From this, you can sense the profound mysteries of Feng Shui.

The most harmful sha stays in the area where 2 black and 5 yellow appear at the same time. It is best to avoid the use of this area. Otherwise, the person staying there will easily encounter serious trouble. Please do not risk giving it a trial.

2 black and 3 jade meeting in the same area invite sickness and lawsuit. However, if the occupant is a doctor or a lawyer, all this works out for the best. The quality of this combination helps these types of business to prosper instead. No other types of business can survive the presence of sickness and lawsuit qi. How should most people handle these stars? Avoid them or reduce their strength using the five elements.

If 4 green meets 1 white, fame and honor can be the result. But when 4 green meets 8 white, it brings injury to children. To remedy this using Feng Shui, hang a red lantern in that area to dissolve the harmful qi. The child residing there will become lively and healthy.

Students of Feng Shui keep searching diligently and willingly because of their amazement and fascination with this art.

 *Chapter* 7

# Some Remedies Applied to Relieve Negativity Influences

Nowadays, many Feng Shui practitioners love to use wind chimes, fish tanks, mirrors, crystal balls, etc. These articles are recommended by Feng Shui books and have become very popular. They claim that these items are magnificent spiritual medicines for curing Feng Shui problems. Can these medicines cure bad Feng Shui? The answer is: I wish you the best of luck!

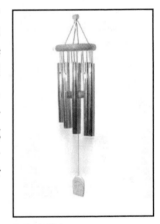

Wind Chimes

### Let's talk about wind chimes.

Wind chimes have a very great effect on Feng Shui. Because of their strong energy, one should not hang them anywhere and everywhere. It may bring negative results if the wind chimes are in the wrong place.

Many Feng Shui practitioners instruct home owners to hang wind chimes in certain places inside the house. Normally, people hear this and do it without any doubts, because they do not understand the advantages and disadvantages of wind chimes.

In ancient days, wind chimes were made of metal.

Feng Shui practitioners would hang wind chimes in a place where the metal element was needed to enhance or to remedy that area. Here, wind chimes were used appropriately.

Consultants from a certain 'school' of Feng Shui use wind chimes here and there, inside and outside of the house, disregarding the principle of harmony. Popular Feng Shui books also teach hanging wind chimes, but seldom warn readers about their negative effects. This is a serious and dangerous misrepresentation.

In my files, I have a record of a lady who was suffering from back pain and other illnesses. She had wrongly trusted a quack, who told her to hang wind chimes in her bedroom. Her illness quickly got worse. Hanging wind chimes was not right in this instance. It brought negative results. In her case, she should have used a fish tank or green water plants. When she added these, her illness improved.

Wind chimes should not be hung randomly. It is extremely important that, in houses with a particular sitting made at a particular time period, wind chimes should never be hung. It would lead to repeated bad luck ending in mental disorders.

A fish tank with plant.

## Fish tank

In places where Chinese gather, one will notice that many restaurants place a fish tank at their entrance. People commonly believe that placing a fish tank in this way will keep money rolling in. This misconception is from the Chinese colloquial saying, "Water means money."

Water placed in the wrong direction will not enhance money, but on the contrary will lessen financial luck.

For example, between 1984 and 2003, water should not be placed in the west. However, if placed in the opposite direction, i.e. the east, it has a good result. In the east, it enhances money luck.

Some say that placing fish in a tank will bring more money, especially the type of fish that are called the "Golden Dragon," or the "Feng Shui fish." This is only a money-making scheme for the one selling the fish. In Feng Shui only the water in the tank is important. The kind and number of fish have no significance whatsoever.

Water, besides producing good money luck, also influences health. On the positive side it reduces pain. However, it can bring disorders to the eyes, heart, and kidneys, as well as blood-related illness.

Bronze indoor water fountain.

A round-shaped mirror

**Mirror**

How should one hang a mirror? Mirrors are commonly used by Feng Shui practitioners. Mirrors come in a variety of shapes and materials - round, octagonal, convex, concave, made of wood or plastic, decorated with the eight trigrams, yin - yang symbol etc.

• **Question**: Can a small mirror have a great effect in getting rid of sha (negative influences in the environment) and overcoming disaster?

• **Answer**: It would be nice if it could, but in reality it cannot.

Generally, Feng Shui practitioners and books say that mirrors can block bad qi, because they reflect it away. This is why you can see mirrors being hung over doors or windows. Whenever a Feng Shui believer feels life is not smooth or health is poor, he will buy a mirror and hang it up, hoping that it will change things for the better.

Those who have deeper insight into Feng Shui know that qi is a type of energy movement. One can direct the movement of energy, but it cannot be reflected. This is a simple scientific truth. A mirror reflects light but it cannot guide the flow of qi.

Today, interior designers employ mirrors in tight or dark areas. This gives the space a wider and more spacious feeling. This is in line with the logic of Feng Shui.

Somebody may tell you that putting a mirror above the stove in your kitchen can immediately improve your money luck. You can give it a try. It will not do any harm.

However, if one has a medical problem, please consult a doctor. Do not gamble your health by hanging a mirror and waiting.

I agree with modern interior design that uses artistic mirrors in conference rooms etc., as a decorative ornament. However, only places like a cosmetics room, bathroom, or rest room need a mirror. Mirrors have no specific meaning in Feng Shui. Their effects, beyond opening up a dark space, are psychological.

An ornate round-shaped mirror

Crystal ball

## Crystal Balls

Crystal balls are the most mentioned tool in western Feng Shui books. Those who practice true Feng Shui understand that the five elements (metal, wood, earth, fire, and water) produce, reduce and dominate one another. Enhancing fortune or dissolving evil is mainly based on the interaction cycles of these five elements. I guarantee that you cannot find a precedent in any ancient Feng Shui books for the use of crystal balls.

This is not to declare that what was not practiced before should not be employed now. However, you have to decide to which element a crystal belongs. The glass mirror has the same problem: to which of the five elements does it correspond?

Feng Shui has detailed theories. The use of metal, water, fire, earth, wood has specific guidelines. If it didn't, and if Feng Shui only depended on mood and intuition, how could this system be passed on from generation to generation with any precision?

Now, how did this false teaching of using mirrors begin? I give a clear answer during my classes. Two of my students, a married couple, have also mentioned this in their publication.

There is still no answer as to how the use of crystal balls crept into Feng Shui. Hopefully, one day some Feng Shui masters can give a clear explanation in a book.

An oval-shape mirror with crystals

*Painted by Larry Sang*

 *Chapter* *8*

# Common Misconceptions
## of Feng Shui

People who are mediocre in Feng Shui believe that a road directly hitting the entrance is never beneficial. Actually, if the qi at the entrance is very strong and very good, it will not be adversely affected by the road. On the contrary the forceful qi brings a more lively qi and makes things thrive. That is why sometimes shops on the corner of a street run a prosperous business: direct qi rushing in from the road can enhance a good entrance.

Of course, if the energy at the door is weak, a road directly hitting it will bring disaster. How to interpret the qi at the entrance is a higher level of study. Not a lot of practitioners are able to understand this point. This subject will not be discussed in detail here.

These mediocre practitioners further say things like: the entrance opening into a staircase, the stove facing the dishwasher, a house located at the end of a dead end street are absolutely unlucky. It is not necessarily so. These are misunderstanding in Feng Shui.

A road directly hitting the entrance.

Entrance opening into a staircase.

*Painted by Larry Sang*

*Chapter* **9**

# Destiny, Luck, and Feng Shui

Those who are versed in Feng Shui should be familiar with the saying that, 'Destiny comes first, luck is second, and Feng Shui is third.' This means that Feng Shui is a helpful technique but has its limitations.

Chinese philosophy teaches that, at the second a life is born, the factor of destiny is fixed. The time, day, month, and year of that moment determine the life's destiny. This is analogous to a car. It may be manufactured as a Honda or as a Mercedes Benz. In astrology, this is the predetermined fate or pre-heaven arrangement, similar to the DNA of a person. The road that this car takes, whether it is a freeway or a country road, at rush hour or late at night, is the second factor, 'luck.'

Feng Shui comes third. It is a supplement to fate. There are limitations placed by an astrological chart. If the astrology does not allow something, Feng Shui can not make it out of nothing. It is the same as an orange tree. The best farmer can never make an orange tree bear apples. Nevertheless, through proper care, irrigation, and fertilization, the farmer can make it bear sweet and juicy fruit.

Furthermore, if fate allows a five-gallon container, then without the assistance of Feng Shui, it may accumulate only three gallons or even less. Here Feng Shui can support and expand the bounty a person receives up to its maximum five gallon capacity.

As an example, I am of a small build, standing only 5feet 2 inches and weighing 110 pounds. There is no way to turn me into the size of NBA's Michael Jordan, no matter how much I want to play basketball.

To explain this in a simpler way, take television as an example. If the picture in the television has snow and is blurred, perhaps it is because of incorrect positioning. After installing a more powerful antenna aimed in the right direction, all is well. However, there are some prerequisites for a good picture. First, the TV must be a good brand and in working condition (fate). Second, the broadcast must be on the air (luck). Third, the antenna must be high enough and in the correct position (Feng Shui).

Feng Shui can help to improve one's life to a certain extent. It can maximize the good aspects and minimize the bad ones, but it can never wholly change the destiny that is predetermined for a person.

If a Feng Shui practitioner tells you that he can use Feng Shui to change your fate and make you a billionaire, he must be selling snake oil.

Having accumulated years of experience, I notice that there are often coincidences that cannot be explained. Those who are in a period of good luck can easily move into a house that is good for money and good for people. On the contrary, a person in a period of bad luck usually lives in a house that is bad for money and bad for people.

Whenever you are down on your luck, Feng Shui can definitely offer assistance and help to rectify the situation. The problem is how to find a good Feng Shui guide. Before employing a Feng Shui practitioner, please do some in-depth investigation. Do not choose one based solely on price.

From experience, matters that are destined can not be

avoided through Feng Shui. The event will happen one way or the other, but Feng Shui can make a big event small. Here is an example:

In early 1990, Mrs. Wang came to my office to have an astrology reading using Ziwei Dou Shu.

Ziwei Dou Shu is a kind of Chinese astrology. Since it was developed in the early Song Dynasty (960-1279), it has a long history of over 1,000 years. It has a very high degree of accuracy. Experts in Ziwei Dou Shu can even pinpoint a toothache by this method of calculation.

During the reading I found that the Tian Tong star transformed to trouble ( 天同化忌 ) in the spouse palace of Mrs. Wang. It signified that trouble would appear between the husband and wife between June 6th and July 6th of that year. I told Mrs. Wang about it and pointed out that the case was not serious. Feng Shui could dissolve it.

She invited me to read her house, which sits south and faces north. The flying stars 2 yellow, 4 green, and 7 red arrived together into a significant place. This combination revealed that the husband would attract 'peach blossom.' (Peach blossom, in this context, means love outside the marriage.) I told her to put a miniature stone landscape in the living room, so it would look like a decorative item. In fact, it was a decorative item used to alter the situation through Feng Shui. The display, when made of the earth element, can dispel peach blossom.

One day, in September, Mrs. Wang telephoned me. Crying, she said that her husband took a mistress recently and had mentioned divorce. She begged me to help her. I remembered clearly that I had taught her to prevent this foreseen trouble early in the year. Why did it still happen?

Actually, the relationship between Mrs. Wang and her husband was excellent. Her husband was proper in every way. Although I had warned Mrs. Wang, she paid no attention. She did not put a stone landscape in the place I indicated.

Early that summer her husband had employed a young woman on his staff. The relationship developed rapidly. They fell in love. Mr. Wang suggested divorce. After Mrs. Wang told me everything, she questioned whether the situation could be mended. I told her to do what I had instructed before: she should put an artificial landscape in the southwest area of her living room without further delay. Afterwards, a dramatic change was noted. Her husband quarreled with his girlfriend and went back to Mrs. Wang. They reconciled on good terms, not mentioning divorce any more.

The above example shows a case where the Ziwei Dou Shu spouse palace of Mrs. Wang showed trouble, but not serious trouble. Thus, Feng Shui can rectify and change the mishap into small damage. If signs of death or separation are shown in the spouse palace, even a powerful Feng Shui master cannot reverse it.

*Painted by Larry Sang*

 *Chapter* *10*

# Burial: One of the Five Chinese Arts

Mountain, medicine, astrology, divination, and appraisal by appearance are the common areas study of the ancient scholars. *Mountain* includes the art of a proper burial. Knowing these arts is an advantage in making a livelihood. Therefore mountain, medicine, astrology, divination and appraisal by appearance are generally called the wu shu 五術 - the Five Arts.

The Five Arts were derived from the changes of yin and yang, the trigrams and hexagrams, and are aided by the various cyclical relationships of the five elements. Through the dynasties, scholars have continuously added, corrected, and adjusted their systems to perfect the supporting theories. This helps to relieve people from their difficulties and brings forth fortune. Though thousands of years have passed, the Five Arts are still deeply rooted in the hearts of the Chinese people and have not perished. They must have true principles and a high value to exist for so long.

Among the Five Arts, we include Feng Shui, which seeks an auspicious yin or yang house. *Yin house* means a gravesite for the dead. *Yang house* means a dwelling place for the living.

Some of the requirements of a yin house are beautiful mountains, sparkling water, and a spacious unblocked view. After burial in such a site, the descendants will be intelligent, clever, handsome, elegant, virtuous, wealthy, long-lived, and scholarly. On the contrary, if buried in a valley bordered by bad hills, near a dirty stream, under ground that has been burnt, or in an ants' den, the descendants will be stupid, obstinate, foolish, wicked, poor, short-lived, and inferior.

How can the auspiciousness or inauspiciousness of a yin house influence the living? It is because the dead are of the same flesh and blood as their descendants. Genes are passed from generation to generation. Therefore, the dead are still linked and will influence their descendants.

It is essential that a yin house environment should avoid windy and flooded places. In addition to this, if the site is sitting against a mountain and facing the ocean, the left and right sides embraced by hills, with abundant greenery, and soft soil that is moist, it is a first class site.

Standing at the cemetery, every tomb looks the same, but a skilled master notices differences. By observing the environment, the Feng Shui master can tell you that the coffin has been twisted because of underground 'wind,' or that the coffin has been attacked by white ants or water erosion, etc. From experience we have found that if the skull of the deceased has become occupied by white ants, the descendants will suffer serious migraines. This seems supernatural, but there are supportive cases. Once you see it, you have to believe it.

Yin house Feng Shui class.

Master Sang in class demonstration.

Cemetery

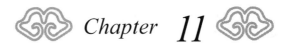 *Chapter* *11*

# Only the Virtuous Can Enjoy
## Good Feng Shui

After many years of research on metaphysics, I firmly believe that only virtuous people can enjoy good Feng Shui. Those who penetrate metaphysics to a high level believe manpower can never conquer nature. No one on earth can reverse qian and kun (heaven and earth). All researchers in metaphysics know that to search for a good Feng Shui house is not an easy task. Even if you find a superior site after a lot of difficulty, you can not guarantee that its surroundings will remain unchanged.

The ancients, besides believing that destiny is the strongest influence, luck is second, and Feng Shui is third, particularly emphasized performing virtuous actions. Nowadays, there are too many practical people who want to take shortcuts in order to succeed. To reach their destination, many would use whatever means necessary, such as profiting themselves at the expense of others, disregarding the virtue of benevolence, etc.

In the end, even if this type of person did employ a good Feng Shui master, paying him an abundant sum, he may still not be able to fulfill his wishes. On the contrary, everything may still go wrong, for example, business failure, etc.

The protecting power of Feng Shui has limitations. I strongly disagree with Feng Shui advertisements in the newspaper, where consultants call themselves great Feng Shui masters, claiming that under their instruction one can become a millionaire. If this were true, shouldn't the one who is advertising become a millionaire himself first?

Further, the bad karma from violating laws, committing crimes, dealing drugs, forcing women into prostitution, and doing evil will not be overcome by the strength of Feng Shui. In the end, if one performs this type of actions, no matter how one tries, using their money to find good Feng Shui, one can not avoid litigation. This is the will of heaven.

The two words, "accumulate virtue," sound superstitious, but this is a very old idea in Chinese society. Those who really know Feng Shui and specialize in destiny, strongly believe that collecting virtuous actions or performing evil deeds will result in auspicious or inauspicious returns respectively. Everything has its own course.

Inherently, a piece of land may be extremely fortunate. However, if an evil-hearted and violent person with ulterior motives gains possession of it, it can become a poor Feng Shui site. There are many ancient Feng Shui stories citing this. Feng Shui can change from good to bad and from bad to good. That is why believers in Feng Shui pay full attention to performing virtuous acts.

## A Story of Bad Feng Shui Changed to Good:

Here is a story about how Feng Shui can turn bad into good. The key character in this story is a mean Feng Shui master. One day in midsummer, he made a long journey and was sweating profusely. He came to rest beneath a huge tree in a village. Not far away, there was a woman washing clothes by a well. The Feng Shui master, Chen Buyi (not the famous master, Lai Buyi) was very thirsty. He begged the woman to give him a bowl of water.

Without saying a word, the woman gave Chen a large bowl of clear water, but she threw in a handful of bran. Chen was very displeased. However, because he was so thirsty, he had to blow away the bran and drink it slowly. After finishing his water, he sat down to talk with the woman.

Learning that he was a professional Feng Shui master, the woman immediately requested Chen to seek a grave site for her father, who had passed away elsewhere. His remains were recently shipped back for burial. Chen, being a mean person, took revenge, because he thought that the woman had put the bran to the water to insult him.

In fact, the woman had been very kind, because after an exhausting journey with copious sweating, one must not gulp cold water quickly. It could bring on sunstroke. The floating bran prevented the quick intake of water.

To make the story short, Chen selected a very bad place, called the "Five Ghosts," for the woman. With his knowledge, Chen knew that after the father was buried in this "Five Ghosts Extinction Site," life would be miserable ever after for the woman's family.

The woman did what she was told, burying her father there. Not too long afterwards, an earthquake occurred. Mountains and land moved. Rivers changed paths. The withered plants and chaotic rocks of the original site became a nice open space at the facing and a strong mountain in the sitting area. It turned into a "Five Ghosts Bring Fortune" site.

The woman's good act turned disaster into fortune, and she gave birth to five obedient sons.

This is a very popular story in Feng Shui. From this story, we understand why our ancestors felt it urgent to point out the importance of bearing a good heart and performing benevolent deeds.

*Chapter* *12*

# Feng Shui and Destiny Depend on Accumulating Virtue

Those who love to investigate metaphysics strongly believe in the principle that "high virtue conveys fortune." As we have seen already, factors in our lives are: 1. Destiny, 2. Luck, and 3. Feng Shui. Destiny and luck can be optimized by Feng Shui. Feng Shui theory is based largely on earth patterns and qi calculation.

Besides geographic influences for fortune and misfortune, there is also a natural force from heaven. If a man seeks for an exquisite site, but he does so for his own profit at the expense of others, if he violates laws, commits crimes, bullies the weak against God's will, then good Feng Shui will not give him divine protection.

## A Story of Good Feng Shui Changed to Bad

In the last chapter, I wrote about a mean-spirited master and a good-hearted woman who turned bad Feng Shui into good. This time I will introduce a story about good Feng Shui changed into bad.

The story occurred at the end of Qing dynasty (ended in 1911), in a wealthy family. The owner died and left a sumptuous fortune and land for his three sons to manage. These three sons each had their own family. The eldest son was greedy, wicked, and treacherous. After the death of his father, being the eldest son, he took over and divided the property into three portions. Needless to say, he took the most fertile fields while the poorer parts went to his brothers.

The father was an earnest devotee of Feng Shui. Years earlier, he employed a Feng Shui master to find a nice grave site. The features were superb, with the so-called 'green dragon' and 'white tiger' protecting the site, and gentle water flowing in. Descendents of the person buried here would prosper.

Yin house not only depends on the environment, but also the erection of a monument is very important. It can spread good fortune equally to every branch of the family or support only one household. The father, of course, wished for everyone to prosper, so he requested the Feng Shui master to place his monument with that goal in mind. However, before burial, the selfish brother privately asked the Feng Shui master to place the monument in the direction that nourishes the eldest son only.

At first, the Feng Shui master refused to act against the father's instructions, fearing that his ethical reputation would be damaged. Finally, he could not resist the money offered to him. In the end, the monument was erected in the direction that only favored the first son's family.

Within two or three years after the burial, bad luck visited the second and third son's homes. They had to sell their property to survive. On the other hand, money was rolling into the first son's family. Everything bloomed for him. The eldest showed no pity on his brothers. Moreover, he bought the property of his brothers, forcing a very low price.

In a short time, nearly all the father's property fell into the eldest brother's hands, except the barren field in front of the father's grave, which belonged to the youngest son. The first son did not want to buy this patch of useless ground. At the end of this disastrous time, the third son sold the land to another party. The buyer re-landscaped the plot, adding shelters, digging fishponds, planting mulberry trees and potatoes, etc.

Problems started to surface. Within a year and a half, 'gold turned into iron,' and bad luck surrounded the first son's family. His business failed. He became involved in crime. Finally, he had to use all his money for bail to avoid being jailed.

Why did these events occur? There is a proverb that says, 'do not use full sails when there is wind.' We believe things should never go to the extreme. One should not count to the last cent. If the eldest son was not so calculating, and had been willing to purchase the barren field, he could have kept all his blessings by not disturbing the grave.

In the front of a burial site, there should be a higher plain called the 'an' or a mesa. The field was this highland, known as 'an tai.' Now, the 'an tai Feng Shui' had been damaged. The first son's family, who received all the blessings, also received all the misfortune. No one would share it with him.

However, the direction of the monument did not influence the livelihood of the second and third son. Poverty soon stimulated their ambition. By and by, their fortune blossomed.

This story shows that one should never be exacting to the last penny. Feng Shui can help to prosper, yet it still requires accumulating virtue in order to enjoy lasting blessings. An evil mind and a harmful heart can turn good Feng Shui to bad.

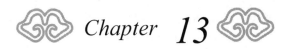 *Chapter* *13*

# Burial in Chinese Culture

Descendants pay respects and show their filial devotion by selecting a fortunate place to bury an ancestor, so that the deceased may rest in peace. This is one of the elegant traditions of Chinese culture.

In old days Feng Shui was of great importance. During the Jin dynasty (265-420 CE), Master Guo Pu began the discussion of the art of Kan Yu (an older name for Feng Shui) and the appraisal of the terrain for burial.

From that far-off dynasty up to the present, there are always many people who value choosing the proper burial ground. When an elderly person passes away, his family will employ a Feng Shui master to select an auspicious plot for burial. It should be high enough, but protected from strong wind; it should not be so low that it is eroded by water. Most important, it must not be invaded by insects. These are the prime requirements.

How can an auspicious site bring wealth and nobility to the descendants? How can the road to fame be passed from generation to generation? On the other hand, how is it that if the deceased is buried in an inauspicious site, the family experiences the following: both wealth and descendants diminish, leaving orphans and widows, members of the family became monks and nuns. This will leave the family without a new generation to carry on the name, which is considered quite a shame in Chinese culture.

From the scientific perspective, to speak of Feng Shui influencing descendants sounds mysterious and arcane. However, the reason behind this belief is logical. Ancestors and descendants are of the same bones, linked together by blood. Therefore, 'waves' are generated that resonate at specific frequencies and waveforms. It is similar to broadcasting from radio and television stations. Recipients using the same frequency can pick up the waves that are emitted through the air.

It is erroneous to believe that Feng Shui is an outdated idea. In Hong Kong, Taiwan, Singapore, Malaysia, America, and Europe, I have a lot of friends and students who are fascinated by Feng Shui. Among them are specialists and professionals in fields such as information technology, design, medicine, engineering, the law, politics, academia, etc.

Of course, those who never get in touch with a skilled master would have a wrong impression. They are misled because crooks and cheaters have contaminated and brought disgrace upon the profession of Feng Shui.

Currently, there are many so-called masters who, when reading Feng Shui for homes and businesses, teach people to hang wind chimes, ba gua mirrors, crystals, flutes, and jade ornaments, to mention a few. Those who are well educated can only shake their heads in sorrow when they see Feng Shui being practiced in such a degraded way.

Feng Shui itself is a set of metaphysical rules. Besides knowing the rules and regulations for practice, hands-on experience is a necessity, especially for selecting a burial site. There is a saying that "when yin and yang are off by a hair, fortune and nobility will never be seen." Feng Shui should never be played with lightly.

Actually, selecting an auspicious piece of land is just as difficult as finding a skilled master. It depends on luck and fate, not on the amount of money spent.

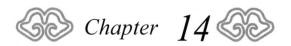 *Chapter* *14*

# The Dragon's Horn or
## the Dragon's Ear?

The scientific world admits that heavenly bodies directly or indirectly affect living creatures on earth. Highly educated people do not dispute this. Those who have a 'scientific' mind but refuse to accept Feng Shui say it is because Feng Shui employs certain 'supernatural' ideas that still can not be verified.

The foundation of Feng Shui is built on yin - yang and five element theory. Through the knowledge of yin-yang and five elements, Feng Shui seeks the way to select, change, and improve the living environment of human beings. The study of yin-yang and the five elements first appeared during the Spring and Autumn, and Warring States Periods (771-221 BCE). Afterwards, these theories became an essential aspect of Chinese culture.

In the early stages, Feng Shui was mainly concerned with yin house. It was only by the end of the Ming and early Qing dynasty (17th century) that reading yang house became popular.

From the old days until now, there have been numerous stories handed down and widely discussed among the common people. There are as many Feng Shui stories as there are as grains of sand in the Nile, and these stories are tinged with mythology. The best place to began, when telling Feng Shui stories, is with Guo Pu of the Jin dynasty (265-420 CE). He was the first grandmaster in this field. The book attributed to him, which is essential for all practitioners to read, is the "Book of Burial."

Guo Pu, who was also known as Jing Chun, was born in Wenxi, Shanxi Province, and was extremely knowledgeable. He was the best author of poems and verses in his province. He was also highly knowledgeable in yin - yang and five element theory, and specialized in the art of Feng Shui. His fame spread far and wide.

For this story, you should know that mountains are often called the 'dragon' because their form resembles a sleeping dragon. Areas of a mountain may be described as a body part or the dragon, such as the head, the tail, etc.

Emperor Ming of the Jin Dynasty loved Feng Shui. He had heard a lot about the miraculous work of Guo Pu and took a liking to him. Once he heard that Guo Pu performed a reading for a local family. The emperor could not suppress his curiosity, and changed into a disguise of civilian clothes in order to see the gravesite that Guo Pu had chosen.

Emperor Ming was a habitual student of Feng Shui. At the grave site, he saw that Guo Pu had selected the 'horn of the dragon.' According to an old book called "Qing Wuzi's Book of the Tomb," if one is buried at the dragon's horn, soon wealth will rise explosively, but later the family will be destroyed.

The Emperor thought Guo Pu, being so famous, should not have selected such a bad site, and wondered whether he held a grudge against the deceased's family. He could not keep silent, and lowered his dignity to enquire, "Why was your ancestor buried at the dragon's horn? Are you not afraid of your family's destruction?" The head of the family laughed: "What's on the dragon's horn? It's the dragon's ear. You did not learn enough. Please do not assess a deer as a horse."

Emperor Ming's curiosity rose and he asked, "Buried at the dragon's ear!?! What will happen?" The head of the family firmly answered, "Master Guo ordered us to bury our ancestor at this good dragon's ear site. Within three years our fortune will be to reach the Emperor."

When Emperor Ming heard "reach the Emperor" he was shaken and desperately asked, "That means after three years, you shall become the Emperor?" He immediately asked how long had the ancestor been buried.

The descendant replied: "Already three years. But you have misinterpreted the phrase 'reach the Emperor.' It does not mean to become the Emperor. It means the Emperor shall come here to visit in person." Emperor Ming felt relief and whole-heartedly admired the accuracy of Guo Pu's prediction.

The above is only one of the many prevailing Feng Shui stories. I shall tell you another amazing one in the next chapter.

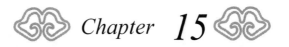

Chapter 15

# Guo Pu's Grave Site

In the previous chapter we talked about the miraculous skills of Guo Pu. Being so, it is logical that the gravesite he picked for himself should be the most auspicious and fortunate place of all to nourish his descendants. To our surprise he had no successor to carry on his abilities. His offspring were without renown.

Traditionally, it is said that a person with good fortune will be buried in an auspicious site, and that an auspicious site serves only the fortunate. According to my experience, when people go searching for houses during their time of good luck, even a house casually picked will generally not have bad Feng Shui. On the other hand, people who are in their unlucky period of time, somehow, will either choose a bad Feng Shui house or the deal for a good house will not go through.

It is even more spooky when selecting a grave site. No matter how carefully it is planned, if an affinity does not exist between the person and the ground, there will be mishaps to prevent burial at that particular chosen site. It is beyond belief!

In 1999, I was presenting a Feng Shui seminar in Guam. Two faxes arrived simultaneously from Los Angeles from two different law offices regarding the same case. Both the claimant and the defendant wished to employ me on their behalf in court as a Feng Shui expert.

The reason for this legal case was that the cemetery management had wrongly buried a person in a site already sold to another couple. When the husband visited the grave of his wife, he found the portion reserved for him was already occupied. He brought the case to court. Under my persuasion and advice, both parties agreed to settle out of court.

From this, you can see that peculiar things can happen. If the husband is fortunate enough, perhaps because of this mistake, he can find a better gravesite. On the contrary, even if prearrangement is made for a fortunate plot, it could end up like this case. One way or the other, unanticipated events may result in burial in the wrong place.

Let's go back to Guo Pu. According to the record, during the Qing dynasty (1644-1911 CE), a Daoist visited the tomb of the famous Feng Shui master, Guo Pu. The grave site was at the foot of Gold Mountain, in a suburb of Jiangsu Zhen. It faced a fast-flowing river, with gusty wind, huge waves, heaps of rocks and boulders, and was covered by moss. It was definitely not a good burial place. It broke all the rules of the "Burial Classic," which states that valuable ground should be smooth. Ground with rough rocks cannot be used as a burial site. This poor site of Guo Pu puzzled a lot of people.

A book, published in Ming Dynasty (1368-1644), gives a clue. Although Guo Pu was a nationally renowned Feng Shui master, he had a very rebellious son. If he said 'east,' his son would go west. Whatever he said, his son would do the opposite. As a father, Guo Pu knew his son thoroughly and decided to tackle the problem psychologically.

Guo Pu selected a first-class gravesite that would promote riches, longevity, fame, and fortune for his descendants. The place was near the peak of Gold Mountain, but he deliberately ordered his son to bury him at the foot of the mountain.

Because his son always contradicted him, Guo Pu thought by saying this his son would bury him at the top of the mountain.

However, everything has its own course and destiny. Pre-arrangement could not win over pre-heaven. After the death of Guo Pu, the son deeply regretted his past behavior: not listening to his father, not performing his filial duty as an obedient son. To amend his faults, the son decided to follow his father's will and so he buried Guo Pu at the foot of Gold Mountain.

Guo Pu's careful planning went in vain. Affairs conflicted with wishes. His descendants declined. This is an example of the Chinese philosophy that a person with good fortune is buried in an auspicious site. It is not necessary to strive for it.

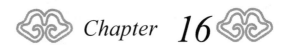 *Chapter* $16$

# The Effects of Cremation

After death, is it preferable to be buried underground or to be cremated? This is a very common question.

In the big cities of Southeast Asia, a lot of people choose cremation. It is even more common in the United States and Canada. In Feng Shui, there are pros and cons. Cremation is simple and tidy. Just select a good direction to house the jar of ashes and everything is settled. It is said a body, after cremation, no longer induces auspicious or inauspicious effects in its descendants. This is unlike ground burial, where one must seek an auspicious site, and pick a date and time to perform the ceremony. Furthermore, the changing of the time periods has to be considered

The reasoning against cremation is mainly based on traditional cultural beliefs, i.e.: one should "rest peacefully underground." Some presume that after cremation, the descendants' nature tends to be fierce and vehement because of the fire.

Actually, the advantages and disadvantages of cremation versus burial depend on the individual's views and needs. In regards to whether or not the descendants receive auspicious or inauspicious effects after cremation is a point worthy of discussion.

In 1989, I attended the funeral of a friend's father. The deceased, after cremation, was buried in a cemetery. The site sits geng (247.5 - 262.5°) and faces jia (67.5 - 82.5°). The time period was seven (1984 - 2003).

The geng to jia direction calculation for period seven gives us an 'up the mountain and down into water' configuration. It is a 'reversed' star and time, a situation of defeat. Even worse, that year the three sha rested in the east, at the facing of the gravesite. (Sha is a negative influence in the Feng Shui qi or environment.) According to Feng Shui theories, this is not an acceptable site.

I felt very uncomfortable. Nevertheless, I understood that my friend had consulted a local Feng Shui practitioner to select the grave site while I was out of town.

Within two years, ill fortune occurred repeatedly. First, my friend's only son drowned in the swimming pool at home. This was followed by divorce. Then his business violated a law and had to declare bankruptcy.

Another case that involves cremation regards a tomb that sits xun (127.5 - 142.5°) and faces qian (307.5 - 322.5°). The year was 1994, when the 5 yellow star arrived in the center. This is also a 'reversed house,' which is very inauspicious. Not long after burial, one of the descendants died in a car accident.

There are many other similar cases where the burial of cremated ashes has obvious effects on the descendants. This is why I believe that there is a certain induction of effects between the dead and their descendants, even after cremation.

Earth burial is more specific than cremation. Besides putting full attention to the orientation of the grave site, choosing the right day to perform the ceremony is also significant. People who want to get rich by taking short cuts can take this opportunity to 'fight the three sha.' One picks a certain date to direct this course, but it is dangerous, and the side effects can cause a lot of harm.

Yin house Feng Shui not only influences believers, it can also affect those who do not have faith in its power.

I have inspected a lot of different tombs in Southeast Asia. In the Philippines, the tombs of the rich are more luxurious than the houses of the average person. In comparison, the tombs in Indonesia are far more plain and simple.

I go to Taiwan two or three times each year. It is peculiar to notice that, in the cemeteries at Danshui, there are a lot of tombs built during this current seven period (from 1984 to 2003). All of them sit jia (67.5 - 82.5$^{\circ}$) and face geng (247.5 - 262.5$^{\circ}$). Buried here are important people from the political and business sectors.

According to the rules of star calculation in Feng Shui, there are six poor positions which wither wealth and descendants during period seven. Sitting jia facing geng and the opposite are two of the six.

Taiwan is a place where people strongly and earnestly believe in Feng Shui. Such an expensive cemetery that buries prestigious people would not have neglected consulting a Feng Shui master. I wonder if the master they consulted used a compass to read the sitting and facing of the grave sites. I do not agree with his choices.

Finding good Feng Shui is governed by luck. Money is not the issue.

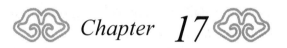 *Chapter* *17*

# The Influence of
## Yang House Feng Shui

We have discussed several cases for yin house readings. Now let's talk about yang house. Actually, Feng Shui is not so far off that it cannot be touched. In other words, it can be analyzed logically step-by-step. General speaking, people spend three-quarters of their life in the house, in activity or resting. One can imagine how important the house is for well-being. Feng Shui acknowledges the visible and invisible influences on the house which affect the physical body and the mind.

One reason Feng Shui is ridiculed is because there is so much mysterious terminology: 巒頭 luan tou (mountain head), 理氣 li qi (texture of qi), 青龍 qinq long (green dragon), 白虎 bai hu (white tiger), 赤雀 chi que (red bird), 玄武 xuan wu (black tortoise), etc. Why don't we simply say the features of the mountains and streams, the flow of qi, left, right, front, and back, respectively? Aren't these easier to understand and less complicated?

The setting of the house, lighting, materials used, color combinations, temperature, and humidity all have a definite influence on those who live inside. These are all essential factors in modern home design. The average person just does not pay much attention to their surroundings.

The study of Feng Shui, besides concentrating on the above factors, puts additional stress on the year of construction, and the sitting and facing direction of the house. Based on calculations, we find the areas of the beneficial qi and the harmful qi. We use the qi flow to lessen, dissolve, or improve the energy, resulting in greater benefit from the living environment for the residents. This is not superstition.

The most important influence on a person is destiny. Second is luck. The third influence is Feng Shui. Feng Shui is a way to balance destiny and luck. Within certain limitations, it can improve luck. But, if handled incorrectly, it may make things worse. However, Feng Shui can never turn a fool into a genius.

Time is a witness to Feng Shui. It has lasted thousand of years without withering. It surely must have a potential. Even though there are unexplained aspects, in actual practice, Feng Shui is repeatedly validated. This leads to belief without further doubt. Seeing is believing.

In 1991, a lady visited me and told me that she was pregnant. In the past she had suffered four miscarriages. The doctor diagnosed the case as 'habitual miscarriage.' He said that unless she immediately started bed rest, she might not be able to save the baby. Being an executive for a company, it was impossible for her to keep away from the office for the full length of her pregnancy. Her friends recommended her to seek assistance from Feng Shui.

I went to investigate her house. It was constructed in the sixth period (1964-1983), sitting si (between 142.5 and 157.5$^\circ$) and facing hai (between 322.5 and 337.5$^\circ$). The master bedroom was in the northeast.

Using the 'flying star' calculation, I found that the northeast was harmful for children. This bad qi could easily be neutralized. I instructed the lady to put a small lamp with a red shade beside her bed. She should light it before going to bed. This use of the fire element was based on the flying star chart of the house. It is not a generic cure for miscarriage. In her case, the outcome should be hopeful, if she used it.

After that, the lady went to work as usual. She did not change her lifestyle. After nine months, she gave birth to a plump and pretty little girl.

Her husband, a French man, loved her dearly, but did not believe in Feng Shui. A year later, the lady got pregnant again. The doctor told her that she was healthy, and the pregnancy was stable. Based on the previous success, the doctor believed she could safely have another baby.

After the birth of the first baby, her husband had removed the red lamp, as he found it displeasing to his eyes. This time, since the doctor said that it was a healthy normal pregnancy, the couple did not place the Feng Shui red lantern near the bed.

A curious thing happened. Without any warning, she suffered another miscarriage. Since then, the French husband is a strong believer in Feng Shui.

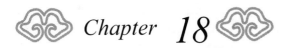

*Chapter* *18*

# Feng Shui is Professional Knowledge

Classical yang house Feng Shui theory is based on matching the living environment to activities of the human being, and feeding their spiritual and physical needs. Precious experience collected over thousands of years, gathering statistics, and case studies have developed into what we today call Feng Shui or the study of the environment for people.

Feng Shui is neither complicated nor unfathomable. With the exception of qi, scientific explanations and proofs exist regarding Feng Shui: the study of the facing and sitting directions, the environmental setting, the five elements (i.e. metal, wood, water, fire, earth), lighting, temperature and humidity, etc. All of the above are considered essential aspects of architectural design.

Feng Shui is sneered at because many crooks are involved in Feng Shui. They advertise widely through the media and use the name of Feng Shui to grab money. On the other hand, those who have profound knowledge in Feng Shui 'treasure their own feathers' and do not seek publicity. This phenomenon creates some confusion. Should one believe in Feng Shui? People hope Feng Shui brings them luck, while on the other hand are afraid that they may get cheated and hurt.

Those who cheat using the name of Feng Shui damage others and themselves as well. All who have the desire to study destiny, face reading, and Feng Shui believe that every action has its results. Life is a shallow bucket for those who practice false Feng Shui, select grave sites by just babbling 'left green dragon, right white tiger,' speak of devils and spirits, past lives, and use ghosts and gods to cheat. Many of this type of charlatan lead a rotten life, surrounded by bad luck. It is because they have cheated.

*Painted by Larry Sang*

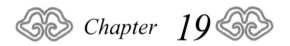 *Chapter* *19*

# A Case Study of a Mistake by an Inferior Feng Shui Master

I was introduced to a Mr. Cai at a wedding feast. Mr. Cai, who resides in Monterey Park, California, was a good friend of the host.

Eight months earlier, under the guidance of a Feng Shui master, he bought a house. The master picked a date, and Mr. Cai moved in. Mr. "Feng Shui" believed that Mr. Cai, a "west group" person, was well-matched with this "west group" house. He also instructed that the front door should not be used, but they could enter by the back door on the left side. He told Mr. Cai to place a red talisman by this door, and to hang a sword and a crystal ball in the living room.

Unfortunate things happened one after the other once Mr. Cai and his family moved in. First, his only son became side-tracked, involved in trouble at a nightclub, and was convicted of a crime. Then, his wife died after being seriously hurt by a robber while shopping at a supermarket. Within a short time, less than a year, a normal family encountered such dramatic changes. The host of the party introduced me to Mr. Cai, hoping I could go to read his house.

After chatting with Mr. Cai, I felt that he was an honest and humble person, so I agreed to have a look. The next day, at appointed time, Mr. Cai sent his chauffeur to pick me up.

His house was sitting wei (between 202.5 and 217.5°) and facing chou (between 22.5 and 27.5°). It was built in 1982.

The front door was in the northeast section. Nevertheless, under the poor guidance of Mr. "Feng Shui," he used the west door as his entrance. If you have studied the flying stars, you can check this for yourself.

An educated Feng Shui master would know at a glance that the house was built in a bad location – "up the mountain, down in the water," or reversed stars. In addition, the terrain was poor. It must bring poor fortune and disaster to its occupants.

Worst of all, Mr. Cai was misled by the inferior master to use the door in the west section. That is where the 2 black and the 5 yellow stars were located. The 2 and the 5 together is an extremely poor combination. It brought serious damage, especially to the female owner.

Due to the poor location of the house, even a competent master could not overcome all the difficulties. However, the mishaps could have been avoided. It was destiny that led Mr. Cai to believe an inferior master and to use the 2-5 entrance. I suggested Mr. Cai reposition his bed, use the main entrance, block the west door, and put the metal element in the 2-5 section.

In the end, Mr. Cai sold the house and moved elsewhere. This unfortunately is a common situation, where harm is caused by a bad Feng Shui master.

*Painted by Larry Sang*

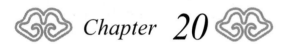

*Chapter* 20

# An Interesting Feng Shui Story

A famous Feng Shui master told me this story:

There was a department store in Guangzhou. The boss, Mr. Zhou, was a great believer in Feng Shui. For the grand opening, he employed a local well-known Feng Shui master to read the store.

On arrival, the master took out his compass to measure the sitting direction. He used his fingers to do the calculation, based on the construction year of the building. He remained deep in thought for a while, and then exclaimed, "This is a good Feng Shui house that invites money for twenty years. You can make a profit. However, you must stay alert next month. There will be an accident that leads to death."

Mr. Zhou was shocked. He quickly begged for a remedy. Was he himself going to be the victim of this fatal disaster? The master said, "Let's see. Give me your birth date and time, and also the birth data of your employees. I will perform some calculations to see who is destined for this ending."

That evening, Mr. Zhou, without any delay, gathered the birth information of his staff. Together with his own, he passed it to the Feng Shui master.

The next day, the first thing Mr. Zhou did was to inquire who had this bad destiny. To his surprise, the Feng Shui master commented, "After careful calculation, none of your staff, yourself included, has this problem."

Mr. Zhou hastily asked, "Then how can you say that there will be a death here next month?"

The master answered: "This I can not explain, but the calculation can never be wrong. To be on the safe side, tell your staff to be careful next month."

Time passed. One afternoon in the following month, Mr. Zhou was working in his office. Suddenly, he heard an uproar outside. Mr. Zhou went to see what had happened. An aged couple had come shopping, and without any warning, the old man had a heart attack. He passed out on the floor and died. Later, the ambulance arrived and took the body away. This death was exactly as predicted.

Here ends the story. Readers might ask, "Does Feng Shui really has such high ability to predict the future?"

As for me, I do not believe that the prediction was based purely on calculation. But by using Feng Shui to determine auspicious or inauspicious locations and timing, plus other kinds of Yi Jing calculations such as Huo Zhu Lin (Fire Pearl Forest), one can definitely foretell the future with shocking accuracy.

*Painted by Larry Sang*

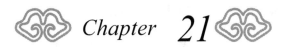 *Chapter* *21*

# The Mystery of Chinese Astrology

In Europe and America, Feng Shui has become as popular as the martial arts and Shaolin Gongfu. More and more people talk about Feng Shui with great relish. Many universities and institutes have supplementary courses, using a modern scientific approach to research and calculate statistics, to rigorously test and examine the truth of Feng Shui.

The background of 5,000 years of Chinese culture includes Confucianism, Buddhism, Daoism, and the Yi Jing, along with the types of metaphysics derived from it. Of all of these, Feng Shui is the most able to coexist with the powerful current of history until today in East Asian culture.

Men put their own safety and wealth as the first priority, followed by the welfare of others, society, and then finally the country. To learn metaphysics is to seek methods of prediction. In this way, by choosing a suitable place and time, one can change the variables to turn disaster into felicity, pursuing a good future and shunning the course of calamity. The ability to predict is the most highly desired knowledge for human beings.

Handed down for thousands of years, and encountering tremendous changes from dynasty to dynasty, the development of metaphysics has branched out into different schools, with abundant varieties of prediction in astrology. I can name a few. However, to the English reader, most of these names are meaningless. The names are as mysterious to the average Chinese as they are to the English-speaking person. Here are the names of some of the schools or styles of astrology:

Ziwei Dou Shu (Purple Emperor Constellation Calculation),

Ziping Si Zhu (Ziping's Four Pillars),

Guo Lao Xing Zong (Guo Lao Star Ancestor),

Tai Yi Shen Shu (Great Yi Miraculous Calculation),

Tie Ban Shen Shu (Iron Board Miraculous Calculation),

Qi Men Dun Jia (Extraordinary Gate to Escape Jia),

Mei Hua Yi Shu (Plum Flower Yijing Calculation),

Liu Ren Shen Shu (Six Ren Miraculous Calculation).

The most common schools in Feng Shui field are Ba Zhai (Eight Houses), San Yuan (Three Time Periods), and San He (Three Combinations). As for face and palm reading, there are also an assortment of schools, each having its own specialties and levels of accuracy.

Every school of Chinese metaphysics has its own mysterious power. Things are often not believable unless experienced. Face and palm reading, divination, astrology, Feng Shui: no matter which art you pick to pursue as a career, you can make a living doing it. Maybe you won't become a billionaire, but you can be well fed and clothed.

*Painted by Larry Sang*

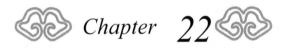

*Chapter* *22*

# Iron Board Miraculous Calculation

Among the numerous schools in Chinese metaphysics, the most renowned, enchanting researchers, is Tie Ban Shen Shu (Iron Board Miraculous Calculation) also known as Huang Ji Shen Shu (Highest Extreme Miraculous Calculation). This school of metaphysics is kept highly confidential. If not handed down by a real master there is no way to enter. There are very few scholars who are well versed in "Iron Board."

In the Far East many gentry, wealthy merchants, politicians, and celebrities have their life calculated by Iron Board Miraculous Calculation. They love to talk about how precise it is.

There is a book named *Amazing Talk About Iron Board Miraculous Calculation*. In it, there is a vivid description of the reaction of the famous Hong Kong science fiction writer, Ni Kuang, who was bewitched by this method's 100% accuracy. Ni Kuang is scientifically oriented, and is a complete skeptic for things like ghosts and spirits. Fascination and disbelief stunned him, and he became obsessed with one question, "Is man really born with a pre-set destiny? Or, could this book have come from another planet?"

I am a lover of metaphysical research. A golden opportunity appeared and I was able to learn the secrets of Iron Board Miraculous Calculation. This brought me to another level of life. I was bestowed with the blessings of Iron Board Miraculous Calculation. Now, no matter where I go, arrangements are made to house me in the executive suit of a five star hotel, and I am entertained enthusiastically with fine wine and exquisite food. On the other hand, I suffer from its fame. Every trip I take, I can not return home as planned, because more friends of friends beg me for a reading. I can not reject them totally. It is definitely true that there is no rose without thorns.

*Painted by Larry Sang*

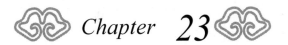 *Chapter* *23*

# The Accuracy of Iron Board

It was said that Iron Board Miraculous Calculation (Tie Ban Shen Shu) started in the Song dynasty (960-1279), originating from the Yi Jing scholar, Shao Kangjie. It became popular in the Qing dynasty (1644-1911) and was handed down until the present. Nevertheless, only a few have true knowledge in this area.

There is a strange phenomenon in Chinese metaphysics. Although it is flooded with swindlers who lack real qualifications in every area, no one who pretend to be an Iron Board Miraculous Calculation scholar. This is because one has to describe a person's past and present life in such precise detail, that no one could fake a reading.

Generally, those who practice Iron Board have a higher income than practitioners of other areas. A friend read a magazine article about a man who was willing to pay a large amount of money to a master to learn this skill, but was rejected. He asked me if this could be true, or if it was exaggerated. We will not discuss its reality or overstatement here. I also had an offer to pay me an even larger honorarium to become my apprentice with a goal of learning my secret knowledge. Holding firmly to my own reason and principles, I gracefully refused him. Even though this was a huge amount of money, it would be a good investment. In Taiwan "telling destiny" is a hot item. A conservative estimate shows that, within a year, this student's principal plus interest could have been doubled.

Iron Board Miraculous Calculation is the utmost in mystery. After listing the correct birth year, month, day, hour, and minute, a calculation will give a complete account of the closest relatives. It is like counting family treasures. Generally, it will tell:

(1) the animal sign of the parents, if they are alive or deceased, or separated;

(2) the numbers of brothers and sisters, their ages or animal signs, and whether they are from the same parents or step parents;

(3) the year of marriage, the age and animal sign of the spouse, if the person will be married once, or the number of marriages. The year of separation will be told, if applicable;

(4) any sons or daughters, and their birth year;

(5) the health status, including if there will be surgery, and how many times;

(6) past luck;

(7) future luck.

Here, I will quote a little from a reading that was sitting on my desk:
- The father is a tiger; the mother is a dragon; this must be so;
- The parents separated; misfortune fell onto the children;
- There is a father and a step-father;
- No sisters; an only daughter;
- Three younger brothers;
- She is graceful and elegant;
- She is frank, but has a tender nature;

- Sometimes she is clever; sometimes stupid; not silly, but actually foolish;
- Her wealth is like a thousand peach leaves; beautiful, but not solid; early flowers, late fruit;
- Many drinking friends, but few true friends;
- Her early life is like a flower in a mirror and the moon reflected in water; her later luck comes from heaven;
- At 25, she married; her husband is a dragon; it lasted 7 years; this is fate;
- At 36, she remarried; her husband is a monkey; this marriage is fixed; they will have daughter, but lack a son;
- At 27, she gives birth to a girl;
- At 38, she gives birth to a girl;
- Lucky in the east; unlucky in the northwest;
- Before 25, she lived under the blessing of her parents;
- From 26 to 40, she starts to taste the bitter side of life; sweet and bitter mixed;
- At 41, mistrusted sweet tongue; wastes a lot of money;
- At 42, her husband died;
- At 43, golden flask, wealthy flower; ... Golden flower on the rock; (shortened)
- At 55, she fights to win; it is as she wished;
- At 56, she digs out jade; gets gold from the sand; (shortened)
- From 75 onwards, piles of gold and silver; lots of luxurious places; her late luck is like a fragrant orchid; non-stop.

This is an extract from an Iron Board Miraculous Calculation reading. What makes it distinctive is the 100% accuracy of the animal signs of the closest relatives, the marriage information, and the years of giving birth. It then briefly talks about the past, and stresses the future, eight pages in all. This is a complete perfect statement of Iron Board Miraculous Calculation.

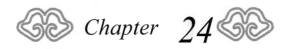 *Chapter* *24*

# Divulging Heaven's Will

After thousands of years of development, Chinese metaphysics has developed into various schools. Each school is unique and has its own specialties and shortcomings.

Regardless, the aim of each type of metaphysics is to predict the future. By using different interpretations, Chinese metaphysics can calculate the earth's luck, the country's fortune and the rise and fall of human endeavors. Generally speaking, metaphysicians can directly calculate the future. Nevertheless, all masters warn their pupils not to 'divulge the will of heaven.' This is because skilled metaphysicians believe that if one knows too much, has too much exposure, if their skills are too dazzling, and they do not keep a low profile, they may easily invite jealousy from heaven. Although fear of 'divulging heaven's will' looks superstitious, it contains a rationale. However, quacks take this "leaking heaven's will" as a shield to fend off problems that they do not know how to solve.

Some who seek advice from metaphysicians hide things that made them lose face. They think that they can hide the truth. When these secrets are not mentioned by the metaphysician, they may think that he is unqualified. This is entirely wrong. The metaphysician may not reveal private matters that could cause embarrassment.

For example, in Iron Board Astrology, there are simple

clear phrases that may hurt one's self-esteem. I have experienced a lot of these cases. The wife of a renowned merchant came to me to read her life. One of the phrases from the reading said, "at age 42, secret love affairs, a public husband and a hidden husband."

Another newly married woman came. The reading for her love life proclaimed, "married five times to reach eternity." How can one spell out these phrases and put them down in writing?

The phrases in Iron Board Astrology can be very straight forward, for example:

"Rich but merciless, will get ill luck in the end,"

"Easy-going sexuality, destined for immorality,"

"Stealthy love, like sister-in-law in the morning, and like wife in the evening."

These words concern personal privacy. The master can never speak out this type of truth. He will receive his own bitterness if he does. I always tell my students that it is difficult to calculate metaphysics, but the most difficult part is letting the client knows about inauspiciousness that is seen in the reading. How can one phrase an upcoming disaster in a way that the client understands, and leads him to be courageous in facing the future? This somehow may help to override the problem.

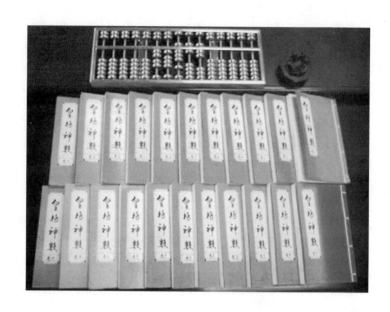

The Tools for Iron Board Calculation

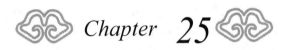 *Chapter* 25

# Plum Flower Yi Jing

It takes a long time to calculate one's life destiny by Ziwei Dou Shu, Four Pillars, Guo Lao Xing Zong, and Iron Board astrology. If you are in a hurry to know about a matter, the success or failure of a business, whether a wish will come true or not, etc., there are additional ways to find out within a few minutes. Their accuracy always stuns the audience. Da Liu Ren, Qi Men Dun Jia, Yi Jing divination, measuring words, etc. are this type of calculation. Yi Jing divination can be further divided into Jing Fang Yi Divination and Plum Flower Yi Jing.

It is rumored that the Plum Flower Yi Jing was written by Shao Kangjie of the Song Dynasty. In the preface of an old copy of Plum Flower Yi Jing, the legend of this book was told. Shao Kangjie, also known as Shao Yong, was a famous philosopher in Northern Song dynasty (960-1126). He was well versed in Yi Jing and divination. He was wise and diligent since his childhood. Shao Yong had an immense memory. He read the *Four Books* and the *Five Classics* by the age of twelve.

For a time, Shao Yong lived like a hermit, with no heater in winter and no fan in summer. He dedicated himself to learning the Yi Jing thoroughly. He pasted all the hexagrams on his wall, trying to grasp their meaning, but in vain.

One day, after his afternoon nap, a mouse appeared. Shao Yong threw his porcelain pillow at it. He missed and the pillow broke into pieces. In the shards, he found a note that read, "This pillow was sold to a learned man named Kangjie. On certain day, certain month, certain year this pillow will be broken." The date given was exactly the date that this occurred.

Shao Yong was amazed. He went to search for the person who sold him this pillow. The seller told him that the note was written by an old man. So Shao Yong brought the pillow and went to visit this person. He knocked on the door. A man answered, and said that his father had died. However, before his death, the old man had said that on a certain day, certain month, certain year, a scholar would come. He left a book to be given to this person. This would be the person to whom his knowledge should be handed down.

Shao Yong opened the book and was delighted that it was a copy of the Yi Jing, with notes that explained the divinations. Shao Yong followed the instructions and was totally enlightened. From then on, he was able to foretell with such accuracy that earned him the title of "Shao, the half-immortal."

After getting this secret book, Shao Yong enjoyed watching the plum blossoms on his way home. He saw two birds fighting. They knocked some plum branches off the tree. Curious, he made a divination. Based on this, he knew that a girl in the neighborhood would fall from the plum tree while picking flowers. Word of the precision of this prediction spread widely and so the method was called Plum Flower Yi Jing.

*Painted by Larry Sang*

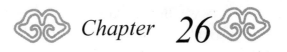 *Chapter* *26*

# Mao Zedong and Feng Shui

In 1997, I was invited by a Chinese bank to present a seminar on the topic of Feng Shui. The audience raised this question: Why did President Jiang Jieshi (Shang Kaishek) of the Republic of China, who keenly believed in Feng Shui, lose control of the nation, while Mao Zedong, who distrusted Feng Shui, come to monopolize the country? Can this be explained?

To answer this question it is necessary to appreciate the thoughts and movements of Mao, including the facade which was known to the public, and also the neglected or purposely hidden side of his life. Mao Zedong was an avid reader, and a student of an assortment of ideas. He loved Chinese literature, and was well-versed in prose and poetry. At an early stage, he opposed the old culture and was clearly prone to materialism. During the Cultural Revolution, he made sure that old traditions were uprooted and suppressed.

Mao Zedong was born in 1893. At that time, Chinese culture was deeply imprinted by the Yi Jing. This highest book of the five great classics was a must for every scholar to study. The Yi Jing, besides discussing philosophy, metaphysics, and calculation, includes yin yang theory and the five elements. These ideas developed into refined details and exquisite theories that lead to specialties such as divination, star and face reading, human destiny prediction, Feng Shui, etc. Learnèd scholars of the old literature could seldom avoid being immersed in this.

Born in this period, and being a voracious reader of books, Mao was no exception. It has been revealed that Mao Duansi, the great-grandfather of Mao, was a first class Feng Shui practitioner. The tomb of Mao Duansi's wife was known as a "dragon head," while that of his son was a "tiger resting plain." Both had been selected on fortune grounds. It was rumored that there was strife in the family over the ground. This strife went so far as a legal appeal. Raised and surrounded by such strong believers in Feng Shui, it was hard for Mao not to be influenced.

The People's Republic of China was founded on the 1st October, 1949, when Mao Zedong felt he was invincible. He believed that "man definitely can overcome heaven." However, from the chosen date and time for the founding ceremony, 3 p.m. on the 1st October, 1949, it is obvious that metaphysics had been taken into consideration.

In normal practice, a founding ceremony would be held in the morning to capture the auspiciousness of morning's brightness and prosperity. On the contrary, it was held in the afternoon. This combines the auspicious date of the 1st October (jia zi) with the xin wei hour. Jia, a wood day, pairs with the xin (metal) hour to give the image of a golden axe, this weapon the main beam to support the country. This implies blessing China and restoring it from hardship so that it can bud into a strong country. Only a super master would be able to choose such an auspicious time. Mao, being a busy person, would not have time to do this himself. Even if he could have personally chosen the date, it is unlikely he would have the ability to choose such an auspicious date without help.

When older, Mao was more fatalistic. In 1975, at the age of 83 he said, "If not at 73, then at 84 King of Death will call upon me." As foretold he died the next year at the age of 84 in 1976.

When Mao was in his military base in Yanan, a skilled master read his four pillars of destiny. The reading disclosed:

> Nobility cannot be described in words;
> The family without assets;
> Enjoying everyone's wealth;
> Fame spreading over the four seas;
> Ten-thousand miles of rivers and mountains all under his rule;
> The red dragon riding a crane goes and does not return.

1976 was the year of bing chen. Bing belongs to red fire while chen represents the dragon. Bing chen means the red dragon. 'Riding on a crane that does not return' hints at the end of life.

All the above could be true but some of it is based on assumption. However, in accordance with Mao's background, and the time of his upbringing, one can question whether Mao himself shunned the five Chinese arts.

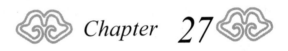 *Chapter* *27*

# Word Analysis I

Word analysis is also called 'breaking words' or 'appraising words.' It is predicting for someone based on the components of a Chinese character that he picks at random. This technique is less common today because the study of word analysis is so immense. The person who predicts based on words must first of all have a wide and solid foundation in the Chinese language. Then he must thoroughly know the eight trigrams, the five elements, Yi Jing, fate calculation, and the four seasons, etc. He must also have worldly experience with various types of relationships. But the most difficult part is that the scholar must have a quick response to "catch the opportunity." It is difficult for a general practitioner to acquire this level of knowledge.

Word analysis is divided into various schools. Basically, there are two types: the highly educated ones and the itinerants. In the old days, those who visited tea houses and wine cellars to find clients were called Spring Outing ( 踏青 Ta Qing). Those who sat on the roadside were called the Pool of the Inkstone ( 硯池 Yan Chi). Those who rented a place and had a permanent address were called Promoting a Yang Place ( 拔陽地 Ba Yang Di). Those who worked inside temples were called Promoting a Yin Place (拔陰地 Ba Yin Di). Those who used the Yi Jing were called Yi Jing Trigrams and Hexagrams ( 易卦 Yi Gua). Those who carried a small wooden box that contained various accessories were called

Viewing the Plum Tree ( 觀梅 Guan Mei).

The skilled ones in the old days were mostly highly educated. They didn't need to do this kind of work for a living, but due to their ego or some kind of dissatisfaction with their life or disliking solitude, they would go to the market place and make predictions for fun.

Word analysis is said to have begun during the Zhou dynasty (1027-221 BCE). It flourished in the Tang (618-906) and Song (960-1279) dynasties. There were also many skilled masters during the Ming (1368-1644) and Qing (1644-1911) dynasties.

Yuan Tiangang, Xie Shi, Li Chunfeng and Shao Yong (Kangjie), etc. were amongst the Tang and Song scholars who practiced measuring words. All of them were great scholars, the walking dictionaries of their time.

Xie Shi was so famous for measuring words, that the Emperor, Song Gaozong visited him, disguised in civilian clothes. Song Gaozong used a stick to write the word 一 (one) on the ground in front of him, and stared at Xie Shi. Xie said, "The one (一) on top of the earth (土) is the King (王)." Xie felt that this person was not a common man.

Song Gaozong wrote another word: 問 (ask). As he was writing on a stony ground, the word was not clear, and half appeared like 君 (monarch). Xie Shi said, "Looking from the left, is the word 君 (monarch). Looking from the right is also the word 君 (monarch). You must be the Emperor." Then he knelt on the ground before Song Gaozong.

Song Gaozong loved Xie's knowledge and invited him to serve the empire. One day the emperor called Xie to his palace. He wrote the word 春 (spring) and asked Xie to calculate the country's fate. Xie Shi bowed and said, "Although a spring ( 春 ) day ( 日 ) is good, the name Qin (秦) is heavy, and oppresses the light of the spring day."

Gaozong was speechless. At that time, the prime minister, Qin Gui (秦檜), was thought by many to betray the country. He had taken over a lot of power and disrespected the emperor. A spy told Qin Gui about Xie Shi's reading. Qin became angry and sent Xie into exile.

On the way to the border, Xie Shi met a girl performing word measure. He had never known a girl to do it. He wrote the word 謝 (his surname, which also means 'thank you'). The girl said, " is made up of 寸 (inch or small), 言 (words), and 身 (body). You are only a low ranking official." Xie Shi paid her homage.

Cheng Yisan of early Qing, was a great scholar and practiced measuring words. He enjoyed his own life and did not seek a political career. His entire life was spent reading words. One day, a client wrotes 玄 (dark, mysterious) to ask about the illness of his son. Cheng Yisan asked the age of the child. The client answered, "five." Yisan said emphatically, "The word 玄 one side of the word for child 孩 The other part is 子 (son). When you wrote the word, you didn't include the image of the son (子). This means that there is no son. If 玄 is divided into the upper part, the middle part and the lower parts, then the upper has part of the word six 六 but is incomplete. The son is now five years old but the incompleteness of six shows an obstruction. The middle part, long-lasting 久 is also incomplete. The lower part, man 人, is too short. This is not a sign for longevity."

The client wrote another word one (一) to see whether there was a chance to save his son. Yisan said, "One the first stoke of the word death 死 and the last stoke of the word life 生. One 一 in Yi Jing numerology is the Kan trigram and belongs to water. This year your son is five years old and five belongs to earth. The child is five years old. Five belongs to earth and dominates one water. The fate of your son can be plainly seen from this. The end will come in less than five days." All that was foretold came true.

From the stories above, you can see the depth of knowledge that is needed. Beside a strong foundation in Chinese writing, you have to know Yi Jing divination, and the five elements as well.

If you are able to show off your skill in word analysis at a dinner party, you will immediately become the star of the evening. My experiences of this sort in Hong Kong and Taiwan were unforgettable.

One year, near the end of the term for President Li, a banquet was held in northern Taiwan. A high ranking government official asked me whether he could become the head of a certain department. He wrote the word 明 (bright). I was able to diagnose clearly, "The sun 日 and moon 月 are bright 明. The sun 日 was written at night, so it gives no light. The moon written on the evening of the thirtieth day of the lunar month is the new moon, dark. I am afraid your wish can not come true." Unfortunately, I pointed directly to the result.

I want to talk about the kidnap case of Bai Xiaoyan, the daughter of Bai Bingbing, a Taiwan celebrity, in the next chapter.

*Painted by Larry Sang*

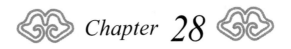 *Chapter* **28**

# Word Analysis II

Word analysis is a special area within metaphysics. The tool it uses is ordinary writing. Word analysis is used to express the idea behind the word.

The essential key in word analysis is to 'catch the opportunity.' That means making use of what you see, what you hear, the rate of movement and the development of the scene around you... all this goes along with feeling and touch. After brainstorming, the underlying meanings of the word will be there.

This is why the same word, asked for different matters, can be either auspicious or inauspicious. Even the same word asked for the same matter can be different when asked by different people. Due to dissimilar situations, the answer can vary from fortunate to bad. A word itself can not be defined as good or bad.

Whether or not prediction comes true depends upon the swiftness, the brightness and the intelligence of the scholar. Inspiration for word analysis should not be based on the handwriting of the client nor the personal opinion of the scholar. This will distort the meaning and the predicted results do not follow. It has to be normal and straight with the components of the word, and tickled by the surroundings. This is how one finds accuracy nearby.

There are a few widely told stories about measuring words. Most lovers of word analysis have heard these tales. Here is one:

One day Shao Kangjie, the famous Yi Jing scholar, was

resting leisurely at home. A client, Zhao Cheng came with a friend. He wanted Kangjie to give a prediction for his son's illness. Zhao wrote the word 字 (word in Chinese character) on a piece of paper. Kangjie diagnosed as, "This word has the top part of the family character 家. Within it there is a son 子, meaning there is a son in the family."

Although the word did not predict when the son would get well, it implied that he should be all right. Hearing this, Zhao was relieved, and took out his pipe to smoke. He lit his pipe with an ember. Unexpectedly, the ember fell on the paper and burnt away the part of the word with 子 (son).

Kangjie frowned and said, "The sickness of your son becomes acute. The situation is not so optimistic. Please look at the word that you have written. In an instant, the fire burnt away the 子 (son) leaving only the mark of fire. It became the word 灾 (disaster). Based in the speed of the fire, I judge that the sickness will develop very quickly." Zhao Cheng was very sorrowful and left. His son recovered, but because of lack of rest, he fell ill again and died shortly.

From the story above, a master of word analysis must know Chinese characters thoroughly, so that he can talk about it precisely.

A lot of people mix up word analysis with divination. This is incorrect. Divination uses the sixty-four hexagrams as the tool to predict, but word analysis is rooted deeply in Chinese learning.

Recently, there has been upsetting news in Taiwan was about the kidnapping of the daughter of Taiwanese celebrity Bai Bingbing. This reckless act of criminals left the police at a loss. Everyone turned pale at the mention of Chen Zhengxing, the leader of the gang. These cunning, savage gangsters caused the police many headaches. They were not caught for a long time. Members of the upper level police force had to resign.

According to my memory, there was an evening banquet in September, that year. I was invited by someone closely related to this case, hoping I could foretell its development and when the gangsters would be caught. I asked the guest to think for thirty seconds and write a word on the paper. He then wrote the word 利 (profit). At a glance, I congratulated the host and said: "The case will soon be closed. One side of benefit 禾 is the (wheat), which shows the image of the harvest. Ripe wheat is harvested in autumn. You wrote this word at the end of September, in the appropriate time. The other side of benefit 利 is the word is 刀 (knife). This is the tool for harvest. Now September is coming to an end, and October will start soon. The case shall be close shortly. Nevertheless, the knife sign gives an unlucky image. I am afraid there will be blood shed.

After hearing this all at the party felt relieved and smiled. Soon after, I went back to California. In mid October one gangster committed suicide and the other got caught. During the capture, one police officer was shot and killed. It was found that, unfortunately, the hostage was killed even before my prediction had taken place. The case was declared closed.

With years of experience, word analysis has a power of clear prediction that is so mysterious. There are so many other examples that could be told.

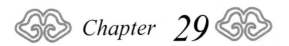 *Chapter* 29

# How to Become A Good Feng Shui Practitioner

Friends and readers often ask me about the criteria and the length of time it takes to become a good Feng Shui practitioner. I usually offer the following response.

1) Seek a mentor with care

Before seeking a mentor, you must first be able to differentiate which Feng Shui mentor has real mastery in Feng Shui. When I say "real mastery", I am referring to a mentor who not only has studied with a famous Feng Shui master, but also he or she has read numerous ancient traditional Feng Shui texts. In addition, this mentor should have practical experience in reading yang house and yin house Feng Shui.

Due to the popularity of Feng Shui in recent years, the bookstore shelves are stacked with a profusion of "how to" Feng Shui books, while the internet and the media are flooded with Feng Shui advertisements. These books on the market have a good demand and a big sales volume; however, the majority of this literature is only teaching Asian folk traditions and beliefs, such as using mirrors, crystal balls, wind chimes, fish tanks, red paint, elephants, Japanese fortune cats, three-legged frogs, etc. This shallow introduction to Feng Shui reflects the authors' limited knowledge in the area. Nonetheless, these writers are holding classes worldwide. If you seek mentorship from such a Feng Shui master, then you are fishing in an empty well.

2) Persistence and Patience

There is no shortcut in Feng Shui. The foundation to Feng Shui includes the study of the He-tu, Lo-shu, pre-heaven, post-heaven, Yi Jing hexagrams, the relationships of the five elements (their productive, reductive and dominating cycles), Luo-pan reading and Xuan Kong calculations. If learning Feng Shui is a spur of the moment fervor, without continuous dedication and determination, then you will have great difficulty in gaining true mastery in this subject.

The study of Feng Shui is like any other study, in that once you have reached a certain level, you will encounter confusion and uncertainty and difficulties will arise. At this time, you must have patience in finding the answer, as well as the humility to seek advice from others. Once you discover the answer, you will enter new level of sophistication. Still, difficulties will arise over and over again endlessly. With each breakthrough you have in finding your answers, you will raise your level of mastery. The greater the mastery you have in Feng Shui, the more excitement and pleasure Feng Shui will bring you, as it becomes an indispensable aspect of your life.

3) Do not be a "jack of all trades and master of none."

After thirteen plus years of teaching, I have the experience of knowing some students who are always the first to attend any new Feng Shui seminars. In an environment where bad Feng Shui masters are abundant, and good ones are rare, students without any ability to differentiate the good from the bad become bewildered by the conflicting information they have indiscriminately absorbed. In the end, their head is filled with chop-suey in the form of Feng Shui facts and myths that they are unable to piece together. Thus, they do not rise to true mastery.

I provide the above advice for my readers and for beginning Feng Shui practitioners to consider. In learning Feng Shui, there are still many other intricate details you must adhere to as well as mistakes that a practitioner should never make. There are too many to list them one by one at this time.

 *Afterword*

# Afterword

The stories in this book were gathered over the past thirty years, from what I have read, heard, seen, and experienced in my encounters with Feng Shui and astrology. Most of the stories were written for a Chinese journal and magazine. Many of them are about real people that I knew and about events documented in my files.

I have only changed the names to protect their privacy. I have gathered these stories together and put them in this book in hopes that it will benefit Feng Shui and astrology aficionados. Even though it is not a book to teach the practice of Feng Shui, it will, nevertheless, provide people with a reference. I also offer it to people with no background in Feng Shui as some interesting and colorful reading.

**Larry Sang**
**Los Angeles**
**February, 2004**

*Painted by Larry Sang*

# COURSE CATALOG

The following is a current list of the courses available from *The American Feng Shui Institute.* Please consult our online catalog for course fees, descriptions and new additions.

| FENG SHUI | | |
|---|---|---|
| **CLASS** | **CLASS NAME** | **PREREQUISITE** |
| FS095 | Introduction to Feng Shui | -- |
| FS101 | Beginning Feng Shui | -- |
| FS101-OL | Beginning Feng Shui – on-line | -- |
| FS102 | Intermediate Feng Shui | FS101 or FS101-OL |
| FS102-OL | Intermediate Feng Shui – on-line | FS101 or FS101-OL |
| FS105 | Sitting and Facing | FS101 |
| FS106 | Additional concepts on facing and sitting | FS201 |
| FS201 | Advanced Feng Shui (2 days) | FS102 or FS102-OL |
| FS201-OL | Advanced Feng Shui – on-line | FS102 or FS102-OL |
| FS225 | Feng Shui Folk Beliefs | FS-201 |
| FS231 | Feng Shui Yourself & Your Business | FS-201 |
| FS235 | Symptoms in a House | FS-201 |
| FS250 | Explanation of Adv. Feng Shui Theories | FS-201 |
| FS275 | 9 Palace Grid & Pie-Chart Graph Usage | FS-201 |
| FS301 | Advanced Feng Shui Case Study 1 & 2 | FS-201 |
| FS303 | Advanced Feng Shui Case Study 3 & 4 | FS-201 |
| FS305 | Advanced Feng Shui Case Study 5 & 6 | FS-201 |
| FS307 | Advanced Feng Shui Case Study 7 & 8 | FS-201 |
| FS309 | Advanced Feng Shui Case Study 9 & 10 | FS-201 |
| FS311 | Advanced Feng Shui Case Study 11 | FS-201 |
| FS312 | Advanced Feng Shui Case Study 12 | FS-201 |
| FS313 | Advanced Feng Shui Case Study 13 | FS-201 & AS101 |
| FS314 | Advanced Feng Shui Case Study 14 | FS-201 |
| FS315 | Advanced Feng Shui Case Study 15 | FS-201 |

| | | |
|---|---|---|
| FS340 | The Secrets of the "5 Ghosts" | FS-201 |
| FS341 | The Secrets of the "San Ban Gua" | FS-201 |
| FS350 | Feng Shui Day Selection 1 | FS-201 & AS101 |
| FS351 | Feng Shui Day Selection 2 | FS-350 |
| FS350 - OL | Feng Shui Day Selection 1          online | AS101 |
| FS351 - OL | Feng Shui Day Selection 2          online | FS-201 & AS101 |
| FS360 | Marriage and Life Partner Selection | FS-201 & AS101 |
| FS375 | Introduction to Yin House Feng Shui | FS201 |
| FS401 | Preparation for Yin House Feng Shui | FS201&250 & AS101 |
| FS451 | Yin House Feng Shui (4 days) | FS401 & Exam |

## YI JING

| | | |
|---|---|---|
| YJ101 | Beginning Yi Jing Divination | AS101 |
| YJ102 | Yi Jing Coin Divination | AS101 |
| YJ103 | Plum Flower Yi Jing Calculation | AS101 |

## CHINESE ASTROLOGY

| | | |
|---|---|---|
| AS101-OL | Stems and Branches Online | -- |
| AS101 | Stems and Branches | -- |
| AS102 | Four Pillars 1 & 2 (Zi Ping Ba Zi) | AS101 |
| AS103 | Four Pillars 3 & 4 (Zi Ping Ba Zi) | AS102 |
| AS201 | Zi Wei Do Shu Astrology (3 days) | AS101 |
| AS680 | Iron Board Astrology | Hand Selected by Master Sang |

## CHINESE ASTROLOGY

| | | |
|---|---|---|
| CA101 | Palm and Face Reading 1 & 2 | -- |
| CA102 | Palm and Face Reading 3 & 4 | CA101 |
| CA103 | Palm and Face Reading for Health | -- |
| CA121 | Introduction to Chinese Medicine | -- |

## CHINESE PHILOSOPHY

| | | |
|---|---|---|
| CP 101 | Introduction to Daode Jing | -- |

**Classes at the American Feng Shui Institute**:

Due to limited seating capacity, reservations are necessary and seats are on a first come first serve basis. To reserve your seat, a $50 deposit is required and is non-refundable if cancellation by student takes place less than three days before class. Please mail-in a check or call us to reserve your seat with a credit card. Balance is due on day of class.

Graduates may repeat these classes for $15.00 per day, if seating is available. Please contact the Institute during the week of the class

**On-Line classes with the American Feng Shui Institute feature:**

* Easy navigation
* Self tests at the end of each module
* A discussion board with trained Institute instructors
* Audio Clips for pronunciation
* An online discussion board
* An "Instant Feedback" final exam

The on-line classes are self-paced study modules. They are segmented into four, one-week lessons that lead you at your pace, over the four-week course. You have 60 days to complete the course work. For more information, please see our web page:

http://www.amfengshui.com/classes/olfaq.htm.

You may register at anytime On-Line, or by phone or fax.

Tel: (626) 571-2757
Fax: (626) 571-2065

fsinfo@amfengshui.com
www.amfengshui.com

Address:
108 N. Ynez Avenue, #202
Monterey Park,
CA 91754 USA

Please do NOT e-mail credit card information as this is not a secure metho

**As a Student of the American Feng Shui Institute:**
You will receive a certificate of completion from the American Feng Shui Institute, for the Beginning, Intermediate and Advanced Feng Shui classes. Please do not confuse this with certification or licensing, as there are no requirements for practitioners at this time.

As a student of the Institute, we are available to assist you with your study. We have an online Bulletin Board for questions and answers, featuring a topic search. You will obtain access to the Bulletin Board upon completion of the Advanced Feng Shui class. Due to the complexity of the courses, Graduates may repeat any class that you have already taken, for $15.00 per day, pending available seats. Please see our online course catalog for the most current course offerings. In addition, if you are located in the Southern California area, you can become a member of the American Society of Feng Shui. The Society has monthly meetings that focus on continued study through practical Feng Shui readings and question and answer forums.

**Cancellation and Refund Policy:**
 All institutional charges shall be returned to the registrant less a $50.00 cancellation fee, if cancellation notice is received prior to or on the first day of instruction. Any notification of withdrawal or cancellation and any request for a refund are required to be made in writing.

Refunds shall be made within thirty (30) days of receipt of the withdrawal or cancellation notice and refund request.

The institute does not participate in the Student Tuition Recovery Fund (STRF). We are registered with the State of California. Registration means we have met certain minimum standards imposed by the state for registered schools on the basis our written application to the state. Registration does not mean we have met all of the more extensive standards required by the state for schools that are approved to operate or licensed or that the state has verified the information we submitted with out registration form.

## THANK YOU